Summa Theologica revisited

Thomas Aquinas' key theses and conclusions

© 2024, Lord Marc Smeets, Ph.D.

Table of Contents

Intro

"Summa Theologica" also known simply as the "Summa" is one of the most significant works in Christian theology and philosophy. It is a comprehensive systematic treatise that covers a wide range of theological topics.

Thomas Aquinas, a Dominican theologian, wrote the "Summa Theologica" in the 13th century. It was intended to serve as a guide for theologians and students, presenting a logical and systematic analysis of Christian doctrine and moral philosophy. The work is structured in the form of questions and answers, with Aquinas posing questions and providing responses based on theological reasoning, scriptural references, and philosophical arguments.

Aquinas's approach to theology was characterized by a combination of philosophical reasoning, theological insights, and the integration of classical philosophical ideas, particularly from Aristotle. He sought to reconcile faith and reason, demonstrating that they are not in conflict but rather complement and enhance each other.

The "Summa Theologica" addresses various subjects, including the existence and nature of God, the relationship between faith and reason, the nature of the human person, ethics, the sacraments, and the role of Christ in salvation. Aquinas drew from a wide range of sources, including Aristotle's philosophy, Church Fathers, and his own profound reflections.

Although Aquinas wasn't able to complete the entire "Summa Theologica" during his lifetime, the work remains one of the most influential theological texts in history. It has significantly shaped Catholic theology and continues to be studied and referenced by theologians, philosophers, and scholars of various Christian traditions.

His work has had a significant impact on the development of Christian theology, ethics, and metaphysics. Many consider him one of the greatest theologians and thinkers in the history of Christianity.

The Nature and Extent of Sacred Doctrine

Aquinas begins by discussing whether sacred doctrine is a science, and he argues that it is indeed a science because it involves a systematic study of truths revealed by God.

Aquinas explores the nature of sacred doctrine by examining its subject matter, which is God. He explains that sacred doctrine primarily deals with God Himself, His attributes, and His relationship with creation. It also involves the study of things related to God, such as creatures, moral principles, and the means of attaining eternal happiness.

Moreover, Aquinas highlights that sacred doctrine is based on divine revelation, which is communicated through Scripture and tradition. He emphasizes the importance of faith in understanding and accepting these divine truths. While reason can assist in elucidating and defending the truths of sacred doctrine, it is ultimately faith that provides the foundation.

Aquinas then discusses the relationship between sacred doctrine and other sciences. He acknowledges that sacred doctrine surpasses all other sciences because it deals with supernatural truths that surpass human reason. However, he also recognizes that there can be a harmony between sacred doctrine and other sciences, as both are directed towards seeking truth.

The Existence of God

Thomas Aquinas addresses the existence of God. He begins by posing the question of whether God's existence can be demonstrated, and he proceeds to provide five arguments, often referred to as the Five Ways, as evidence for the existence of God.

The first way is the argument from motion, which asserts that since everything in the world is in a state of change or motion, there must be a First Mover who initiates and sustains all motion without being moved by anything else. This First Mover is what we call God.

The second way is the argument from efficient causality. Aquinas argues that in the world, things are caused by other things, and there must be a First Cause that sets everything in motion without itself being caused by anything. This First Cause is God.

The third way is the argument from possibility and necessity. Aquinas explains that things in the world exist and cease to exist, but there must be something that exists necessarily, without depending on anything else for its existence. This necessary being is God.

The fourth way is the argument from degrees of perfection. Aquinas observes that things in the world possess varying degrees of qualities, such as goodness, truth, and beauty. He argues that there must be a being who possesses these qualities to the maximum degree, and that being is God.

The fifth way is the argument from finality. Aquinas notes that natural objects in the world act with a purpose, as if directed towards an end. He suggests that there must be an intelligent being that directs all things towards their respective purposes, and that being is God.

Aquinas presents these arguments as rational demonstrations for the existence of God, although he acknowledges that they are not conclusive proofs for everyone. He argues that faith is still necessary for a complete understanding of God, as His essence and attributes transcend human reason.

The Simplicity of God

Aquinas begins by explaining that God is supremely simple because He does not have any composition of matter and form, essence and existence, or potentiality and actuality. Unlike created beings, which are composed of different elements and possess various attributes, God's essence and existence are one and the same. He is pure actuality, without any potentiality.

Aquinas argues that God's simplicity is necessary because any composition or division in God would imply imperfection. If God were composed of parts, those parts would either limit His perfection or contribute to His perfection, both of which are contrary to the nature of God as the absolute and perfect being.

Moreover, Aquinas explains that God's simplicity is the foundation for His other divine attributes. Since God is simple, all of His attributes—such as His goodness, wisdom, and power—are not distinct from His essence but are identified with it. Each attribute expresses a different aspect of God's simple and infinite nature.

Aquinas also addresses objections to the simplicity of God, such as the apparent complexity in the world or the use of analogical language to describe

God. He clarifies that while we may use complex terms or analogies to speak about God, it does not mean that God is actually composed or complex in His essence.

The Perfection of God

Aquinas begins by discussing the meaning of perfection and asserts that God is the ultimate standard of perfection. All perfections found in created beings are derived from and participate in the divine perfection of God. Unlike creatures who possess limited and imperfect perfections, God's perfection is infinite and absolute.

Aquinas examines various attributes of God that reflect His perfection, such as His goodness, truth, and unity. He explains that God's goodness is the source of all goodness in the world, and His truth is the foundation of all knowledge and wisdom. God's unity signifies His indivisible and undivided nature, free from any potential contradictions or limitations.

Furthermore, Aquinas addresses objections to God's perfection, particularly those based on the presence of evil and imperfections in the world. He argues that evil is not a positive existence but rather a lack or privation of goodness. Any perceived imperfections in the world do not detract from God's perfection but rather demonstrate His wisdom and providence in allowing for a greater good to arise.

Aquinas also explores how God's perfection relates to His other attributes, such as His eternity, immutability, and simplicity. These attributes further emphasize the unchanging and complete nature of God's perfection.

The Goodness of God

Aquinas begins by affirming that God is fundamentally good in His essence. His goodness is not something separate from Him, but it is His very nature. God's goodness is infinite, perfect, and the source from which all other goodness in the universe is derived.

Aquinas argues that God's goodness is manifested in His works, both in creation and in the governance of the world. God's creative act is an expression of His goodness, bringing into existence a universe that reflects His wisdom, beauty, and order. Additionally, God's providential care ensures the ongoing sustenance and governance of creation, directing it towards its ultimate purpose.

Furthermore, Aquinas explains that God's goodness is not limited to benevolence but also encompasses justice. God's justice is the perfect harmony of His goodness, ensuring that His creatures receive what is due to them according to their nature and the divine order.

Aquinas also addresses the problem of evil in relation to God's goodness. He argues that evil is not directly caused by God but arises due to the misuse of free will in creatures. However, God's goodness is demonstrated through His ability to bring about a greater good even from the existence of evil.

From a human perspective, Aquinas highlights that our ultimate happiness and fulfillment lie in aligning our will with the divine will and participating in God's goodness. By seeking and embracing the good, we can grow in our likeness to God and ultimately attain union with Him.

The Unity of God

Aquinas begins by explaining that the unity of God is unique and unparalleled. Unlike created beings, who are composite and made up of various parts, God is pure act without any potentiality. This means that God is fully actualized and lacks nothing, making Him completely unified in His essence.

Aquinas further argues that God's unity is not only in His essence but also in His existence. God's existence is not derived from any external source or combined with other elements. Rather, God's existence is self-existent and necessary. He is the ground of all being and the source of existence for all things, and His unity is inseparable from His existence.

Additionally, Aquinas addresses the concept of the Trinity in relation to the unity of God. He explains that while there are three persons in the Trinity—Father, Son, and Holy Spirit—they are not three separate gods but rather three distinct relations within the one God. The unity of God is not compromised by the distinction of persons within the Trinity.

Aquinas emphasizes that the unity of God is essential to understand His nature and attributes. It is through His unity that God is capable of being the ultimate source of all perfections and the cause of all things. Furthermore, our knowledge and understanding of God are derived from His unity, as it allows for a coherent and consistent understanding of His divine attributes.

The Infinity of God

Aquinas begins by explaining that God's infinity is not to be understood in the same way as quantitative infinity, which is a potentiality without limit. Rather, God's infinity is understood as a transcendent perfection that surpasses all limits and bounds. It is an attribute that signifies the fullness and perfection of His being.

God's infinity is reflected in various aspects. Firstly, God is infinite in His essence, meaning that He has no limitations or boundaries in His nature. His essence is not restricted by time, space, or any other finite constraints. He is unlimited and unrestricted in His being.

Secondly, God is infinite in His existence. His existence is necessary and eternal, without any beginning or end. He is the ultimate source of existence for all things and does not depend on anything else for His being. His existence is unbounded and infinite.

Thirdly, God is infinite in His perfections. He possesses all possible perfections in the highest degree. His wisdom, power, goodness, and other attributes are infinite and beyond measure. He is not subject to any deficiency or limitation in His qualities.

Aquinas emphasizes that God's infinity does not imply a quantitative multiplication or division, as He is not composed of parts. Rather, His infinity is a qualitative perfection that transcends all finite measurements and limitations.

Understanding the infinity of God helps us recognize His greatness, majesty, and transcendence. It reminds us that God is beyond our comprehension and surpasses all finite realities. His infinity invites us to approach Him with awe, reverence, and humility.

The Eternity of God

Aquinas begins by distinguishing between two types of time: "before" and "after" in relation to moments and succession. He explains that God, being the Creator of time, is not subject to it. Rather, God is beyond time and exists in an eternal present. For God, there is no past or future but only an eternal now.

God's eternity is characterized by His unchangeable and timeless nature. He is not affected by temporal succession or the passing of moments. Instead, He encompasses all moments of time in a single eternal act of existence.

Aquinas further argues that God's eternity is not to be understood as an infinite extension of time, but as a simultaneous possession of all moments. God transcends time altogether and is not bound by its limitations.

Understanding the eternity of God has several implications. It means that God has always existed and will always exist, without any beginning or end. His existence is not contingent upon time but is necessary and unchanging. Furthermore, God's eternal nature allows Him to have perfect knowledge of all events in time, as His timeless perspective encompasses all moments.

Aquinas also addresses the question of human participation in God's eternity. He argues that while humans experience time in their earthly existence, they can participate in God's eternity through their souls, which have the capacity for an eternal union with God.

The Immutability of God

Aquinas argues that God's immutability stems from His perfect and infinite nature. As a being of pure actuality, God has no potentiality to change. He is already in the highest state of perfection and lacks nothing that could be added or diminished. Therefore, there is no possibility for God to undergo any change or alteration.

God's immutability is also related to His eternity. Since God exists outside of time and is not subject to its succession, He remains constant and unchanging in His being throughout all moments of time. His immutability is grounded in His eternal and timeless nature.

Furthermore, Aquinas explains that God's immutability does not imply a lack of action or interaction with the world. While God's essence remains unchangeable, His effects and actions in the world are observed as change. However, these changes are not due to any change within God Himself but are the result of His unchanging will and providence acting upon the mutable world.

Understanding God's immutability has important implications. It assures us of God's reliability and constancy in His promises and attributes. God's unchangeable nature provides a solid foundation for our trust and faith in Him. It also highlights His transcendence and distinction from the changing and transient nature of the world.

The Divine Knowledge

Aquinas begins by asserting that God's knowledge is not acquired or derived from external sources but is innate to His nature. God's knowledge is comprehensive and exhaustive, extending to every detail of reality. He knows all things with perfect clarity and certainty, without any possibility of error or ignorance.

Furthermore, Aquinas distinguishes between two aspects of God's knowledge: His knowledge of Himself and His knowledge of all created things. God's knowledge of Himself is immediate and intuitive, as He perfectly understands His own essence and attributes. His knowledge of created things, on the other hand, is mediated through His divine intellect and encompasses the entire created order.

Aquinas also addresses the question of God's foreknowledge and human free will. He argues that God's knowledge of future events does not diminish human freedom or render human choices predetermined. Rather, God's knowledge is timeless and encompasses all moments of time in a single eternal now. He knows how every individual will freely choose, and His knowledge does not coerce or determine human actions.

Additionally, Aquinas discusses the distinction between God's knowledge of what is necessary and what is contingent. God knows all things that necessarily exist, as well as all things that depend on His creative will. He knows all possible outcomes and contingencies, and His knowledge is not limited by human limitations or uncertainty.

Understanding the divine knowledge has profound implications. It assures us of God's omniscience and wisdom, as He possesses perfect knowledge of all things. It also highlights the harmony between God's knowledge and human freedom, affirming that God's knowledge does not undermine our ability to make genuine choices.

The Divine Will

Aquinas begins by explaining that God's will is closely linked to His intellect. God's will is always directed towards what He knows to be good and desirable. Since God's intellect is perfect and infinite, His will is likewise perfect and unerring. God's will is not subject to any external influences or passions but is grounded in His own intrinsic goodness and wisdom.

Furthermore, Aquinas distinguishes between God's antecedent and consequent will. God's antecedent will refers to what He wills in itself, considering the intrinsic goodness of an object or action. God's consequent will, on the other hand, takes into account various factors and circumstances, such as the choices and actions of human beings. Aquinas explains that God's consequent will is flexible and adjusts according to the choices made by His creatures while remaining consistent with His antecedent will.

Aquinas also discusses the relationship between God's will and His providence. God's providence refers to His active guidance and governance of the created order towards its ultimate purpose. Aquinas asserts that God's will is intimately connected to His providence, as He directs all things towards their proper ends in accordance with His divine wisdom and goodness. Everything that occurs in the world is ultimately guided by God's will, even though it may involve the free choices of individuals.

Understanding the divine will has profound implications. It highlights the perfection and goodness of God's will, which is always directed towards what is truly good and desirable. It also emphasizes the compatibility between God's will and human freedom, as God's will accommodates the choices and actions of His creatures. Additionally, recognizing God's providential will assures us of His guidance and care over the created order.

The Divine Providence

Aquinas begins by addressing the question of whether there is such a thing as divine providence. He argues that the order and regularity observed in the natural world, as well as the fulfillment of specific ends in nature, point to the existence of a providential plan. Furthermore, the existence of intelligent beings with free will, such as human beings, necessitates divine providence to direct and guide their actions towards the ultimate good.

Aquinas distinguishes between two types of divine providence: general providence and special providence. General providence encompasses God's governance of the entire created order, from the movements of the celestial bodies to the operations of nature. It ensures the maintenance of order and the fulfillment of the natural ends of creatures. Special providence, on the other hand, pertains to God's care for individuals, taking into account their specific needs, circumstances, and moral choices. Special providence is intimately connected to God's knowledge and will, as He guides each individual towards their ultimate purpose and destiny.

Aquinas also addresses the question of divine permission, particularly in relation to the existence of evil and human suffering. He explains that God, in His wisdom, allows certain evils to occur for the sake of a greater good. While God permits evil, He is not its cause, as evil arises from the misuse of free will or the disorder in creation. God, in His providence, can bring about good even from evil circumstances, working towards the redemption and salvation of His creatures.

Understanding divine providence helps us recognize God's active involvement in the world and His care for every aspect of creation. It assures us that there is a purpose and plan underlying the events and experiences of our lives. Divine providence also invites us to trust in God's wisdom and goodness, even in the face of challenges and suffering, knowing that He can bring about good from all circumstances.

Evil

Aquinas begins by discussing the nature of evil, asserting that evil has no positive existence in itself. Evil is not a substance or a thing; rather, it is a lack or deficiency in the proper order and harmony of things. Evil is a privation or absence of a due good, just as darkness is the absence of light.

Aquinas then explores the causes of evil. He identifies three types of causes: the primary cause, which is God; the secondary cause, which is the free will of rational creatures; and the instrumental cause, which refers to the physical or material factors that can contribute to evil. God, as the primary cause, does not will evil directly, but He permits it for the sake of a greater good or as a consequence of the free will of rational beings.

Aquinas further distinguishes between two types of evil: moral evil and physical evil. Moral evil is the result of human choices that deviate from the moral order, such as acts of injustice, violence, or deceit. Physical evil refers to the suffering, pain, and disorder present in the natural world, such as natural disasters or diseases. Aquinas explains that physical evil can be a consequence of the limitations inherent in the created order.

Regarding the question of how God can allow evil to exist, Aquinas argues that God's allowance of evil is justified by the greater good that He brings about through it. God can bring about good even from evil situations, working towards the redemption and perfection of His creation. He allows evil to exist to respect the freedom and responsibility of rational creatures, and to manifest His justice and mercy.

Aquinas concludes that although evil exists, it does not have ultimate power or victory. God, who is supremely good and just, is capable of bringing good out of every evil situation. Evil, in the grand scheme of God's providential plan, is a means through which a greater good can be accomplished.

The Divine Power

Aquinas begins by establishing that God's power is infinite. Since God is the ultimate source of all being and perfection, His power is unrestricted and knows no limits. God's power is not limited by anything outside of Himself, and He can bring about any possible effect.

Aquinas then examines the relation between God's power and His essence. He argues that God's power is identical to His essence. In other words, God's power is not something separate or distinct from His essence but is an essential attribute of His being. Everything that is in God is God Himself, and His power is an expression of His very nature.

Furthermore, Aquinas distinguishes between God's absolute power and His ordained power. God's absolute power refers to His ability to do anything that is logically possible and does not contradict His own nature. His ordained power, on the other hand, pertains to the specific order and purpose that God has established in the created world. God exercises His power in a manner that is consistent with His wisdom, goodness, and the order He has ordained.

Aquinas also emphasizes that God's power is not arbitrary or capricious. It is guided by His wisdom and goodness, and everything that God does or allows is ultimately directed towards the fulfillment of His divine plan. God's power is exercised in harmony with His other attributes, such as His justice, mercy, and love.

God's Knowledge of the Future Contingent Events

Aquinas begins by establishing that God's knowledge is perfect and comprehensive. As the source of all being and the ultimate cause of all things, God possesses infinite knowledge of all that is, including past, present, and future events. His knowledge is not limited by time or subject to change.

Regarding future contingent events, Aquinas discusses the different opinions held by philosophers and theologians. Some argue that God's knowledge of the future is based on His eternal vision, where He sees all things in a timeless and complete manner. From this perspective, God's knowledge includes all possible outcomes of contingent events.

Aquinas, however, presents his own position, stating that God's knowledge of the future is not based on a sequence of events or a temporal view. Instead, God's knowledge is based on His eternal and unchanging perspective, which encompasses all things in a single act of knowledge.

Aquinas further explains that God's knowledge is not the cause of contingent events but is rather a reflection of His understanding of the nature of those events and the choices made by free beings. God knows what we will freely choose because His knowledge is not bound by time, and He sees the entire span of human history in a single act of knowledge.

Importantly, Aquinas also addresses the issue of human freedom and how it relates to God's knowledge. He maintains that God's knowledge of our choices does not violate our free will. God's knowledge is not the cause of our choices but is a perfect understanding of the choices we will make based on our free and rational nature.

The Divine Knowledge

Aquinas begins by affirming that God possesses infinite knowledge. As the source and sustainer of all things, God's knowledge encompasses all that has been, is, and will be. His knowledge is not acquired or learned but is intrinsic to His divine nature.

Aquinas discusses the comprehensiveness of God's knowledge, stating that God knows all things, including past, present, and future. Unlike human knowledge that is acquired gradually and limited by time and perspective, God's knowledge is instantaneous and complete. He sees all things simultaneously and in their totality.

Aquinas further explains that God's knowledge is not subject to change or influenced by external factors. His knowledge is independent and unchanging, reflecting His eternal nature. God's knowledge is not affected by the passage of time or the actions of creatures. He possesses perfect understanding and insight into all things, including the deepest thoughts and intentions of every individual.

Moreover, Aquinas discusses the distinction between God's knowledge of things in themselves (knowledge of essence) and His knowledge of things as they exist in particular circumstances (knowledge of existence). God's knowledge encompasses both the general principles that govern all things and the specific details of each individual reality.

Aquinas also addresses the question of whether God knows things through their causes or through His own essence. He argues that God's knowledge is not dependent on causes or intermediaries but is immediate and intuitive. God knows all things by knowing Himself, as His essence contains within it the perfection of all knowledge.

The Goodness and Malice of the Interior Act

Aquinas begins by explaining that every human act consists of an interior act of the will and an exterior act in the world. The interior act refers to the intention, desire, or decision of the will, while the exterior act is the physical manifestation or execution of that intention.

Aquinas asserts that the goodness or malice of an act is determined by the object, end, and circumstances of the act. The object refers to the specific action itself, whether it is intrinsically good or evil. The end refers to the intention or purpose behind the action, whether it aligns with the ultimate good or deviates from it. The circumstances involve the various factors surrounding the act, which can affect its moral evaluation.

Aquinas explains that the ultimate standard of goodness is the conformity of an act to the divine law, which is grounded in God's nature and will. The divine law provides guidance for human actions and directs them towards the ultimate end of human life, which is union with God.

Aquinas emphasizes that the interior act, particularly the intention or will behind the action, plays a crucial role in determining the moral quality of the act. He distinguishes between acts that are intrinsically good or evil, regardless of intention, and acts that derive their goodness or malice from the intention.

According to Aquinas, an act can be morally good only if all three aspects—the object, end, and circumstances—are good. If any one of these elements is evil, it taints the entire act with moral evil. However, he notes that a good intention cannot justify an evil act. Even with a good intention, if the object or the circumstances are evil, the act remains morally wrong.

Aquinas also discusses the concept of human responsibility and accountability for one's actions. He affirms that individuals are responsible for their interior acts and are subject to judgment based on the moral quality of their choices and intentions.

The Goodness and Malice of External Human Actions

Aquinas starts by explaining that external actions are the observable behaviors or deeds that manifest the interior acts of the will. While the interior acts of the will determine the moral character of an action, it is through the external actions that these intentions are expressed and made evident to others.

According to Aquinas, the goodness or malice of an external action is determined by three factors: the object, the circumstances, and the end. The object refers to the specific action itself and whether it is inherently good or evil. The circumstances involve the various factors surrounding the action, which can affect its moral evaluation. The end refers to the intention or purpose behind the action, whether it aligns with the ultimate good or deviates from it.

Aquinas emphasizes that the moral goodness of an action depends primarily on the object. If the object is intrinsically evil, regardless of the intention or circumstances, the action is considered morally wrong. However, if the object is morally good, the action can still be evaluated further based on the intention and circumstances.

Aquinas also discusses the concept of double effect, which arises when an action has both good and evil effects. He explains that an action may be permissible if it meets certain conditions, such as the action being morally good in itself, the intention being good, the evil effect being unintended, and the good effect outweighing the evil effect.

Aquinas addresses the role of conscience in determining the moral quality of actions. He argues that a well-formed and informed conscience is crucial for making moral judgments. A properly formed conscience helps individuals discern between good and evil actions and guides them in making morally sound choices.

Furthermore, Aquinas emphasizes the importance of human laws and the authority of rulers in promoting and maintaining the common good. He discusses the relationship between human laws and divine law, highlighting that human laws should align with the principles of justice and be in harmony with the divine law.

The Will of God

Aquinas begins by affirming that the will of God is an essential attribute of His nature. God's will is not separate from His essence but is an intrinsic aspect of who He is. Aquinas argues that God's will is eternal and unchangeable, for God is immutable and unaffected by external influences.

Aquinas distinguishes between God's antecedent will and His consequent will. God's antecedent will refers to His universal will, desiring the well-being and salvation of all His creatures. However, this does not mean that all creatures will ultimately attain salvation, as God also respects the freedom and choices of His rational creatures. God's consequent will, on the other hand, pertains to His particular will, responding to the specific circumstances and choices made by His creatures.

Aquinas discusses the relationship between God's will and His intellect. He asserts that God's will is not driven by external influences or desires, but rather by His perfect knowledge and wisdom. God's will is aligned with His intellect, which comprehends all things in their proper order and goodness. Therefore, God's will always chooses what is best and most fitting according to His divine wisdom.

Aquinas addresses the question of whether God wills evil. He argues that God does not will evil in itself, as evil is the absence or privation of good. However, God may permit evil to exist for the sake of a greater good. God's permissive will allows for the existence of evil and suffering in the world, but He does not directly will or cause evil actions.

Furthermore, Aquinas explains that God's will is the ultimate cause and source of all things. God governs the world according to His will and providence, directing all things towards their ultimate purpose and the fulfillment of His divine plan. Aquinas emphasizes the harmony between God's will and His wisdom, highlighting that God's will is perfectly ordered and directed towards the highest good.

The Love of God

Aquinas begins by affirming that love is an essential attribute of God. Love is not only an action of God but is inseparable from His essence. God's love is perfect, infinite, and unrestricted, surpassing any human comprehension. It is a pure and selfless love, devoid of any selfishness or deficiency.

Aquinas explains that God's love is directed towards all His creatures. His love encompasses the entire created order, from the lowest to the highest beings. However, God's love is not the same for all creatures. He loves each creature in a manner appropriate to its nature and capacity to receive His love. God's love is particularly directed towards rational creatures, such as human beings, who are capable of a deeper and more intimate union with Him.

Aquinas also addresses the question of whether God's love is conditional or unconditional. He argues that God's love is unconditional, meaning that it does not depend on any external factors or the merits of the creatures. God loves all creatures simply because they exist and are part of His creation. However, the effects of God's love, such as grace and salvation, may be conditioned by certain factors, such as the response of creatures to His love.

Furthermore, Aquinas discusses the effects of God's love on creatures. He explains that God's love is the source of all goodness and perfection in creatures. It is through His love that creatures are brought into existence, sustained, and guided towards their ultimate fulfillment. God's love transforms and elevates creatures, drawing them closer to Himself and allowing them to participate in His divine life.

Aquinas emphasizes that God's love is not a passive or indifferent affection. It is an active and dynamic love that seeks the well-being and happiness of His creatures. God's love is manifested in His providential care, His guidance, and His desire for the salvation and eternal union with His creatures.

The Divine Predestination

Aquinas begins by explaining that predestination is grounded in God's eternal knowledge and wisdom. God, in His infinite wisdom, knows all things, including the future choices and actions of individuals. Based on this knowledge, He predestines certain individuals to eternal life, leading them to the ultimate fulfillment of their purpose and happiness in union with Him.

Aquinas affirms that predestination is an act of God's free will. It is not based on any merit or worthiness of individuals but solely on God's gracious choice. God's predestination is guided by His love and mercy, and it reflects His desire for the salvation and eternal happiness of all.

Aquinas addresses the question of whether predestination contradicts human free will. He argues that God's predestination does not eliminate human freedom. Rather, God, in His infinite wisdom, harmonizes both His divine providence and human free will. He works in and through human choices and actions to accomplish His predestined plan.

Aquinas distinguishes between two types of predestination: predestination to glory and predestination to grace. Predestination to glory refers to God's choice to bring certain individuals to eternal life and the beatific vision of Him. Predestination to grace, on the other hand, pertains to God's choice to bestow His saving grace upon individuals, enabling them to cooperate with His grace and attain salvation.

Furthermore, Aquinas addresses the question of reprobation, which refers to God's decision not to grant salvation to certain individuals. He explains that reprobation is not an active choice or rejection on God's part but a passive decision to withhold the graces necessary for salvation. God's justice is not violated in reprobation, as He does not owe anyone salvation. Rather, His justice is manifested in the just punishment of those who reject His grace and persist in sin.

Aquinas emphasizes that predestination should not be a cause of despair or presumption for individuals. Rather, it should lead to humility and gratitude. Individuals are called to trust in God's providential plan, cooperate with His grace, and strive for holiness in response to His loving invitation to salvation.

The Cause of Sin

Aquinas begins by defining sin as an act that deviates from the order established by God. Sin is an offense against God and a failure to conform to His law. Aquinas categorizes sin into two types: original sin, inherited from Adam and Eve's disobedience, and actual sin, committed by individuals through their own deliberate actions.

Aquinas explores the question of why God allows sin to exist. He asserts that God, being all-good, does not cause sin directly, as sin is contrary to His nature. Instead, sin arises due to the free will of rational creatures, particularly angels and humans. God, in His wisdom and providence, permits sin to occur as a consequence of granting free will to His creatures. Free will allows for the possibility of choosing good or evil, as genuine love and obedience require the freedom to choose.

Aquinas discusses the role of the devil as the instigator of sin. He explains that the devil, originally a good angel created by God, chose to rebel against God out of his own free will. The devil entices and tempts human beings, seeking to lead them away from God and into sin. However, Aquinas emphasizes that the devil cannot force anyone to sin. Ultimately, individuals are responsible for their own actions and choices.

Aquinas addresses the question of whether God's knowledge of future sins implies causality. He argues that God's foreknowledge does not cause human actions but rather follows from His infinite wisdom and knowledge of all things. God's knowledge is not a determining factor in human choices, as individuals still possess free will and are accountable for their own actions.

Furthermore, Aquinas discusses the effects of sin, both on the individual and on society as a whole. Sin distorts the proper order established by God, leading to disharmony, suffering, and separation from Him. However, God's mercy and grace provide the means for forgiveness and reconciliation, allowing individuals to overcome the effects of sin through repentance and conversion.

The Effects of Sin

Aquinas explains that sin disrupts the proper order established by God in various ways. First and foremost, sin damages the relationship between the sinner and God. It creates a separation between the individual and God, as sin is a rejection of God's law and a turning away from His love. Sin hinders the sinner's ability to experience the fullness of divine grace and communion with God.

Sin also affects the individual's internal disposition and moral character. It weakens the will and inclines the person toward further sin. Aquinas describes sin as a form of spiritual sickness that corrupts the soul and diminishes its capacity to pursue virtue and righteousness. The repetition of sinful actions can lead to the formation of vices, which are entrenched and habitual patterns of sinful behavior.

Moreover, sin has social and communal consequences. Aquinas explains that sin not only affects the sinner but also has an impact on others. Sin can harm relationships, disrupt the harmony of communities, and contribute to social injustice. The effects of sin extend beyond the individual and can influence the broader fabric of society.

Aquinas emphasizes the importance of repentance and reconciliation in overcoming the effects of sin. Through sincere contrition and the sacrament of confession, individuals can seek forgiveness and receive God's mercy. The grace of God, made available through Christ's redemptive work, enables individuals to be reconciled with God and restores the possibility of living a virtuous and righteous life.

The Passion of Christ

Aquinas discusses the necessity and purpose of Christ's Passion. He explains that the Passion was necessary for the redemption of humanity from sin. Through his voluntary suffering, Christ offered himself as a perfect sacrifice to atone for the sins of humanity. By taking on the punishment that was due to sinners, Christ reconciled humanity with God and opened the way to salvation.

Aquinas also examines the various aspects of Christ's Passion, including his physical suffering, the shedding of his blood, and his mental anguish. He emphasizes the intensity of Christ's suffering, both in his body and in his soul, as he endured the weight of the sins of the world.

Furthermore, Aquinas discusses the effects and benefits of Christ's Passion. He explains that through his Passion, Christ merited not only forgiveness of sins but also the grace of justification, which enables individuals to be made righteous before God. Christ's sacrifice also serves as an example of perfect obedience and self-surrender to God's will, inspiring believers to imitate his virtues.

Aquinas emphasizes the significance of faith and devotion to the Passion of Christ for the salvation of souls. He encourages believers to contemplate and meditate on the sufferings of Christ, recognizing their role in the divine plan of redemption. By uniting their own sufferings and sacrifices with those of Christ, believers can participate in the redemptive power of the Passion and grow in holiness.

The Gift of Christ's Passion

Aquinas explains that the Passion of Christ is not only a sacrifice for the forgiveness of sins but also a gift that bestows grace upon humanity. Through his suffering and death on the cross, Christ merited infinite merits and graces, which he freely bestows upon humanity. These graces are given to individuals through the sacraments, particularly the sacraments of Baptism and the Eucharist.

The Gift of Christ's Passion provides the means for the forgiveness of sins, the restoration of sanctifying grace, and the infusion of virtues in the souls of believers. It brings about the reconciliation between God and humanity, opening the way to eternal life.

Aquinas also highlights the transformative power of the Gift of Christ's Passion. Through the reception of these graces, believers are enabled to grow in holiness, overcome sin, and strive for perfection. The Passion of Christ becomes a source of spiritual strength and the impetus for living a virtuous life.

Furthermore, Aquinas emphasizes the universality of the Gift of Christ's Passion. It is available to all people, regardless of time or place, and extends to all aspects of human life. The redemptive power of

Christ's Passion can heal, sanctify, and elevate every aspect of human existence, both in the spiritual and temporal realms.

The Effects of Christ's Priesthood

Aquinas explains that Christ's priesthood is superior to the priesthood of the Old Law because it is a perfect and everlasting priesthood. Christ is both the priest who offers the sacrifice and the sacrifice itself, as he offers himself on the cross for the redemption of humanity.

The Effects of Christ's Priesthood can be understood in several aspects. First, through his priestly mediation, Christ reconciles humanity with God. By offering himself as the perfect sacrifice, he atones for the sins of humanity and restores the relationship between God and humanity that was broken by sin.

Second, Christ's priesthood brings about the forgiveness of sins. Through his sacrifice, he obtains the remission of sins for all who believe in him and seek reconciliation with God. Christ's sacrifice is of infinite value, capable of purging all sins and bringing about true spiritual healing and restoration.

Third, Christ's priesthood confers grace upon believers. Through the sacraments, particularly the sacraments of Baptism and the Eucharist, the merits of Christ's sacrifice are applied to individuals. Grace is poured out upon the faithful, enabling them to participate in the divine life and grow in holiness.

Furthermore, Christ's priesthood empowers believers to participate in his redemptive work. Through their baptismal priesthood, all believers share in Christ's royal priesthood and are called to offer spiritual sacrifices to God. They are invited to unite their sufferings and sacrifices with those of Christ, participating in the work of redemption and sanctification.

Finally, Christ's priesthood secures eternal life for believers. Through his priesthood, Christ opens the way to heaven and bestows the hope of eternal salvation. By his resurrection, he triumphs over sin and death, offering the promise of everlasting life to those who follow him.

The Cause of the Incarnation

Aquinas argues that the Incarnation was necessary for the restoration of humanity's fallen state. After the sin of Adam and Eve, humanity was separated from God and unable to repair the damage on its own. Thus, it was fitting for God, out of His infinite love and mercy, to take on human nature and reconcile humanity to Himself.

The primary cause of the Incarnation is the goodness and love of God. God became incarnate to manifest His love for humanity and provide a means of salvation. Through the Incarnation, God demonstrates His desire to be intimately united with His creation and to lead humanity back to Himself.

Another cause of the Incarnation is the fulfillment of God's promises and prophecies. Throughout the Old Testament, God made promises to send a Savior, the Messiah, who would redeem humanity. The Incarnation fulfills these promises and brings about the fulfillment of God's plan for salvation.

Furthermore, the Incarnation is also attributed to the wisdom of God. It is through the Incarnation that God reveals His wisdom and teaches humanity the truths necessary for salvation. By taking on human nature, God is able to communicate His divine wisdom in a way that is accessible and comprehensible to human beings.

Lastly, Aquinas mentions the merits of Christ as a cause of the Incarnation. The merits of Christ's passion and death on the cross are applied to humanity through the Incarnation. By assuming human nature, Christ is able to offer Himself as a perfect sacrifice for the forgiveness of sins and the redemption of humanity.

The Mode of Union of the Word Incarnate

Aquinas begins by affirming that the Incarnation involves a true and substantial union of the divine and human natures in one person, the Son of God. The union is not merely a moral or accidental association, but a real and substantial joining together. The Word, or the Son of God, assumes a human nature without losing or changing His divine nature.

Aquinas explains that this union is brought about through the hypostatic union, which means that the human nature of Christ is united to the divine Person of the Word in a unique and indivisible manner. In this union, the two natures remain distinct but are inseparably united in the one divine Person.

Furthermore, Aquinas clarifies that in the Incarnation, the divine nature does not undergo any change or alteration. It remains eternal, unchangeable, and impassible, while assuming a passible human nature. The human nature assumed by the Word is complete and perfect, consisting of a true body and a rational soul.

Aquinas also addresses the question of how the human and divine operations are attributed to Christ. He explains that although Christ possesses two natures, His actions and operations are attributed to Him as a single person. Both the human and divine activities in Christ's life are harmoniously united and directed by the one divine Person.

Moreover, Aquinas highlights the role of the soul as the principle of human operations in Christ. The human soul of Christ, united to His body, acts as the principle of His human knowledge, human will, and human actions. At the same time, the divine nature of Christ is the source of His divine knowledge and divine operations.

The Birth of Christ

Aquinas begins by addressing the question of Christ's miraculous conception in the womb of the Virgin Mary. He affirms the doctrine of the virginal conception, stating that Christ was conceived by the power of the Holy Spirit without the intervention of a human father. Aquinas explains that this miraculous conception was fitting for Christ, who is both God and man, as it signifies His unique and divine origin.

Moving on to the topic of Christ's birth, Aquinas discusses the place and manner of His nativity. He explains that Christ was born in Bethlehem, as prophesied in the Scriptures, and that He was born in a humble and lowly condition, being laid in a manger. Aquinas highlights the significance of Christ's humble birth, emphasizing His identification with the poor and His mission of bringing salvation to all humanity.

Aquinas also addresses the question of whether it was appropriate for Christ to be born of a virgin. He explains that the virginal birth of Christ served several purposes. Firstly, it signifies the purity and integrity of the Virgin Mary, who remained a virgin before, during, and after giving birth to Christ. Secondly, it demonstrates the power and majesty of God, who can accomplish extraordinary and miraculous works. Finally, it emphasizes the uniqueness and divine nature of Christ, who is born without the stain of original sin.

Furthermore, Aquinas discusses the significance of the angels' announcement and the presence of the shepherds at Christ's birth. He explains that the angels' announcement serves as a testimony to the dignity and greatness of Christ's birth, proclaiming His role as the Savior and the fulfillment of divine promises. The presence of the shepherds signifies that Christ's birth is meant for all people, including the lowly and humble.

The Work of Christ's Life

Aquinas begins by examining Christ's life as a whole, emphasizing the perfection and excellence of His actions. He explains that every aspect of Christ's life, including His words, deeds, sufferings, and miracles, was characterized by the highest degree of virtue and righteousness. Aquinas underscores the significance of Christ's life as a model for human conduct, illustrating the path of perfection and guiding believers toward the attainment of eternal happiness.

Aquinas then proceeds to discuss specific events and teachings from Christ's life. He explores topics such as Christ's baptism, His temptation in the desert, His miracles, His preaching and parables, His institution of the sacraments, and His prayer and fasting. Aquinas provides theological insights and explanations regarding the significance of these events, emphasizing their role in fulfilling the divine plan of redemption and revealing God's love and mercy to humanity.

Additionally, Aquinas delves into the mysteries of Christ's passion and death. He explains the redemptive significance of Christ's suffering on the cross, highlighting the atoning power of His sacrifice and the forgiveness of sins that it accomplished. Aquinas also addresses the resurrection of Christ, emphasizing its importance as the triumph over sin and death, and the foundation of hope for eternal life.

Throughout his discussion of the work of Christ's life, Aquinas emphasizes the unity and coherence of Christ's mission. He demonstrates how each aspect of Christ's life and ministry, from His birth to His resurrection, is interconnected and serves a specific purpose in the divine plan of salvation. Aquinas presents Christ as the perfect mediator between God and humanity, reconciling humanity with God and offering the gift of eternal life through His work.

The Death of Christ

Aquinas begins by explaining that Christ's death was not an ordinary death but a voluntary sacrifice. He highlights the voluntary nature of Christ's death, emphasizing that it was an act of obedience and love towards the Father and a means to fulfill the divine plan of redemption. Aquinas underscores the concept of substitutionary atonement, where Christ, as the perfect and innocent victim, offered Himself on behalf of humanity to satisfy the demands of justice and reconcile humanity with God.

Aquinas further elaborates on the effects and benefits of Christ's death. He explains that through His death, Christ merited the forgiveness of sins and the restoration of humanity's friendship with God. Aquinas emphasizes that Christ's death is the supreme example of love, as it reveals the extent of God's love for humanity and provides the means for salvation.

Aquinas also discusses the manner of Christ's death, focusing on the crucifixion. He reflects on the intense suffering and humiliation that Christ endured, highlighting the depth of His sacrifice and the redemptive power inherent in His crucifixion. Aquinas explains that Christ's death on the cross is significant not only for its salvific effects but also as a symbol of triumph over sin and death.

Furthermore, Aquinas addresses theological questions related to Christ's death, such as whether Christ's death was necessary for the redemption of humanity. He argues that while God, in His infinite wisdom, could have chosen other means of redemption, the death of Christ was the most fitting and effective way to accomplish salvation. Aquinas emphasizes the harmony between divine justice and mercy in the sacrificial death of Christ.

The Effects of Christ's Death

Aquinas explains that Christ's death has various effects that contribute to the redemption of humanity. Firstly, Christ's death is the source of forgiveness of sins. Through His sacrifice, Christ atoned for the sins of humanity and opened the way to reconciliation with God. Aquinas emphasizes that Christ's death is the perfect and sufficient sacrifice that obtains the remission of sins for all who believe in Him.

Secondly, Aquinas discusses how Christ's death brings about the restoration of friendship with God. By His obedience and sacrifice, Christ merited grace for humanity, which enables individuals to be reconciled with God and participate in the divine life. Aquinas teaches that through the sacraments, particularly baptism and the Eucharist, the effects of Christ's death are applied to believers, bringing about their sanctification and union with God.

Furthermore, Aquinas explains that Christ's death is an act of satisfaction for the offense committed against God. In His sacrifice, Christ offers perfect satisfaction to the justice of God, making amends for the disobedience of humanity and repairing the relationship between God and humankind.

Aquinas also highlights the transformative effects of Christ's death on human beings. Through faith in Christ and participation in His death through baptism, believers are united with Christ and share in His victory over sin and death. They are called to imitate Christ's self-giving love and conform their lives to His example.

The Resurrection of Christ

Aquinas affirms the reality and truth of Christ's resurrection, stating that Christ truly rose from the dead on the third day, as attested to by the Scriptures and witnessed by His disciples. He emphasizes that the resurrection of Christ is a central and essential doctrine of the Christian faith.

Aquinas explains that Christ's resurrection has profound implications for humanity. Firstly, it serves as proof of His divinity and the truth of His teachings. By conquering death and rising from the grave, Christ demonstrates His power over sin and death, affirming His identity as the Son of God and the promised Messiah.

Secondly, Aquinas highlights the significance of Christ's resurrection for the salvation of humanity. Through His resurrection, Christ triumphs over sin and death, offering the hope of eternal life to all who believe in Him. Aquinas teaches that by sharing in Christ's resurrection through faith and baptism, believers are united with Him and partake in the new life He has obtained.

Furthermore, Aquinas discusses the effects of Christ's resurrection on the Church and the sacraments. He explains that Christ, in His resurrected state, bestows grace and spiritual gifts upon His Church, which enable believers to live in conformity with His teachings and participate in the divine life. Aquinas also emphasizes the importance of the Eucharist, which is a participation in the sacrifice and resurrection of Christ.

Aquinas concludes that Christ's resurrection is a pivotal event in the plan of salvation. It demonstrates His victory over sin and death, offers hope and eternal life to believers, and bestows grace upon the Church. The resurrection of Christ is a central tenet of the Christian faith, providing assurance of God's power and love, and serving as a foundation for the Christian's hope of resurrection and eternal glory.

The Ascension of Christ

Aquinas affirms the reality of Christ's ascension, stating that Christ, after His resurrection, ascended bodily into heaven on the fortieth day. He emphasizes that the ascension of Christ is a crucial event in the life of the Church and an essential doctrine of the Christian faith.

Aquinas explains that the ascension of Christ has several important implications. Firstly, it signifies the completion of Christ's earthly mission. By ascending into heaven, Christ returns to the glory and majesty that He had with the Father before His incarnation. It demonstrates the triumph of Christ over sin and death and signifies His exaltation and reign as Lord and King.

Secondly, Aquinas teaches that Christ's ascension has implications for humanity. Through His ascension, Christ opens the way to heaven for humanity, leading the way as the "pioneer of our salvation." He brings humanity into a new relationship with God and prepares a place for believers in the heavenly realms. Aquinas emphasizes that Christ's ascension is a source of hope for believers, assuring them of their own future glorification and the fulfillment of their longing for eternal communion with God.

Furthermore, Aquinas discusses the role of Christ's ascension in relation to the Church. He explains that Christ, in His ascended state, continues to exercise His authority and ministry on behalf of the Church. He intercedes for believers before the Father, sending the Holy Spirit to guide and empower the Church in its mission. Aquinas also highlights the sacraments as means through which believers are united with the ascended Christ and share in the benefits of His ascension.

Aquinas concludes that the ascension of Christ is a pivotal event that signifies His exaltation, the completion of His mission, and the opening of heaven to humanity. It assures believers of their future glorification and serves as a source of hope and encouragement. The ascension of Christ is a central aspect of Christian theology, pointing to the ultimate destiny of believers and their union with the glorified Christ in the heavenly realms.

The Cause of Human Redemption

Aquinas begins by discussing the problem of original sin and its consequences for humanity. He explains that due to the disobedience of Adam and Eve, human nature became corrupted, and humanity was unable to repair this rupture on its own. Thus, a remedy was needed to reconcile humanity with God and restore the possibility of eternal life.

Aquinas then delves into the question of why the redemption of humanity required the incarnation of Christ. He argues that the incarnation was necessary for several reasons. First, by becoming human, Christ could offer a fitting sacrifice for the forgiveness of sins. As both God and man, he could bridge the gap between the divine and human realms.

Second, Aquinas explains that through the incarnation, Christ showed humanity the depth of God's love and mercy. By taking on human nature and experiencing the trials and sufferings of humanity, Christ demonstrated God's compassion and desire for our salvation.

Lastly, Aquinas highlights that the incarnation also serves as a model for our own transformation and divinization. Through his life and teachings, Christ showed us the path to holiness and union with God.

The Effects of Human Redemption

Aquinas discusses the effects of human redemption in terms of both the forgiveness of sins and the restoration of the human person to a state of grace. Through his sacrificial death on the cross, Christ merited the forgiveness of sins for all humanity. This forgiveness is extended to individuals who, through faith and the sacraments, are able to receive the fruits of Christ's redemption.

Furthermore, Aquinas highlights the restoration of grace as a result of human redemption. Grace is understood as a participation in the divine life, an infused gift that enables individuals to share in God's own nature. Through Christ's redemptive work, the possibility of receiving and growing in grace is made available to all who cooperate with God's saving grace.

Aquinas also emphasizes the transformative power of redemption in relation to the effects of original sin. Through Christ, humanity is freed from the bondage of sin and its consequences. The effects of original sin, such as concupiscence and the inclination to sin, are not completely eradicated, but through God's grace, individuals are empowered to resist temptation and grow in virtue.

Ultimately, the effects of human redemption are aimed at the eternal salvation and happiness of individuals. By reconciling humanity with God, redeeming it from sin, and restoring the possibility of communion with the divine, Christ's redemptive work offers the hope of eternal life and union with God.

The Grace of Christ

Aquinas asserts that the grace of Christ surpasses all other forms of grace. Christ, as the Incarnate Son of God, possesses the fullness of divine grace, and from his abundance, he bestows grace upon humanity. Through his perfect obedience, sacrificial death, and resurrection, Christ merited the grace that is necessary for human salvation.

Aquinas distinguishes between the grace of Christ as it resides in him personally and the grace that is communicated to the members of his mystical body, the Church. The grace of Christ in his humanity is considered personal grace, while the grace communicated to believers is called habitual grace. Christ's personal grace, united to his divine nature, is the source from which all other graces flow.

Aquinas also discusses the role of Christ as the mediator of grace. He explains that Christ, through his redemptive work, reconciles humanity with God and opens the channels of divine grace. As the mediator, Christ intercedes on behalf of humanity, obtaining grace for us from the Father and imparting it to us through the sacraments and other means.

The grace of Christ operates in the life of believers by sanctifying and transforming them. Through grace, believers are justified, forgiven of their sins, and adopted as children of God. Grace also empowers believers to live virtuously and grow in holiness. Aquinas emphasizes that all the virtues and spiritual gifts bestowed upon believers find their origin and efficacy in the grace of Christ.

The Justification of the Ungodly

Aquinas begins by affirming that the justification of the ungodly is a work of God's grace. It is not something that can be achieved through human effort or merit. He emphasizes that God, out of His mercy and love, freely bestows justification upon the ungodly, forgiving their sins and making them righteous in His sight.

According to Aquinas, the instrumental cause of justification is faith. He explains that faith is necessary for justification because it unites the individual to Christ and allows them to participate in His redemptive work. Through faith, the ungodly person receives the grace of God, which transforms them and makes them righteous.

Aquinas also emphasizes the role of God's grace in the process of justification. He asserts that it is through God's grace that the ungodly person is cleansed from sin and infused with righteousness. This grace, Aquinas argues, is freely given by God and cannot be earned or deserved by any human effort.

Additionally, Aquinas discusses the importance of the sacraments in the justification of the ungodly. He explains that the sacraments, particularly baptism and the Eucharist, are visible signs of

God's grace and instruments through which the ungodly person is justified. Baptism, for example, washes away original sin and incorporates the individual into the mystical body of Christ.

The Effects of Grace

Thomas Aquinas explores the effects of grace. Grace, according to Aquinas, is the supernatural gift of God that enables human beings to participate in the divine life and attain salvation. It is through grace that individuals are transformed and empowered to live according to God's will. Aquinas identifies several effects of grace, which can be summarized as follows:

Justification: Grace is the cause of justification, whereby a person is made righteous before God. Through the infusion of grace, the individual's sins are forgiven, and they are reconciled with God. This justification is a free gift of God, and it enables the person to live in a state of righteousness.

Sanctification: Grace not only justifies but also sanctifies the individual. It brings about a transformation in the person's soul, making them holy and pleasing to God. Grace enables the individual to grow in virtue and avoid sin, leading to a life of holiness and conformity to God's will.

Adoption: Through grace, the individual is adopted as a child of God. They become heirs of God's kingdom and share in the inheritance of eternal life. This adoption into God's family is a profound effect of grace, establishing a filial relationship between God and the individual.

Merit: Grace empowers individuals to merit or earn spiritual rewards from God. By cooperating with God's grace and freely choosing to do good, individuals can accumulate merits that contribute to their spiritual growth and eternal destiny. These merits are not earned solely through human effort but are made possible by God's grace.

Transformation: Grace has the power to transform the individual from within. It brings about a renewal of the person's mind, will, and affections, aligning them more closely with God's desires. This transformative effect of grace enables individuals to grow in virtue, resist temptation, and live a life of charity.

Perseverance: Grace provides the necessary strength and assistance for individuals to persevere in their journey of faith. It sustains them in times of trial, helps them resist temptation, and enables them to remain faithful to God until the end. The gift of final perseverance, which ensures that a person dies in a state of grace, is considered a special effect of God's sustaining grace.

The Merit of Human Acts

Merit refers to the deservingness of reward or punishment based on the moral quality of one's actions. Aquinas examines the concept of merit in relation to grace and highlights several key points:

Divine Merit: Aquinas emphasizes that the primary source of merit is God Himself. God bestows His grace upon individuals, enabling them to perform good actions and merit rewards. It is through the grace of God that humans are empowered to do what is morally good and pleasing to Him.

Supernatural Merit: Aquinas distinguishes between natural and supernatural merit. Natural merit refers to actions performed by human beings on their own, based on their natural abilities and virtues. Supernatural merit, on the other hand, is rooted in God's grace and supernatural virtues infused in the soul.

Meritorious Works: Aquinas identifies certain conditions for human acts to be considered meritorious. Firstly, they must be morally good actions performed with the help of grace. Secondly, they must be done freely and willingly, without coercion. Thirdly, they should be directed towards a supernatural end, such as eternal life or the glory of God.

Reward: Aquinas affirms that God, in His justice, rewards meritorious actions. The reward is not something that humans can claim as a right but is given by God out of His generosity and faithfulness to His promises. The nature and extent of the reward are determined by God's wisdom and justice.

Role of Grace: Aquinas emphasizes that all meritorious acts are ultimately rooted in God's grace. It is God who enables individuals to perform good acts and grants them the capacity to merit rewards. Human beings cooperate with God's grace and freely choose to participate in meritorious actions.

Role of Christ: Aquinas highlights the central role of Christ's merit in the salvation of humanity. Christ, through His passion, death, and resurrection, merited the grace that is necessary for human beings to be justified and receive eternal life. It is through union with Christ and participation in His meritorious work that individuals can merit rewards before God.

The Cause of Merit

Merit refers to the deservingness of reward based on the moral quality of one's actions. Aquinas explores the factors that contribute to the merit of human acts and identifies the following causes:

Grace: Aquinas emphasizes that the primary cause of merit is divine grace. It is through the grace of God that humans are enabled to perform good actions and merit rewards. Grace is a gift freely given by God, and it elevates and transforms human nature, enabling individuals to participate in the divine life and perform actions that have supernatural merit.

Virtue: Aquinas notes that virtues play a crucial role in meritorious actions. Virtues are habits or dispositions that incline individuals to act in accordance with reason and moral goodness. The virtues acquired through the cultivation of moral habits contribute to the moral quality of actions and enhance their merit.

Charity: Aquinas highlights the importance of charity, or the theological virtue of divine love, in meritorious acts. Charity unites individuals to God and enables them to love Him above all things. When actions are performed out of love for God and neighbor, they acquire greater merit.

Faith and Hope: Aquinas also acknowledges the role of faith and hope in meritorious acts. Faith is the theological virtue through which individuals believe in God and accept His revealed truth. Hope is the theological virtue that directs individuals towards the attainment of eternal life. Acts performed in faith and hope, rooted in trust in God's promises, can have meritorious value.

Cooperation with Grace: Aquinas emphasizes that human cooperation with divine grace is essential for meritorious actions. While God's grace is the primary cause of merit, individuals must freely cooperate with that grace by aligning their will with God's will and actively choosing to perform good actions. It is through this cooperation that humans participate in the meritorious work enabled by God's grace.

Aquinas's understanding of the cause of merit underscores the central role of divine grace in meritorious actions. Grace, along with virtues such as charity, faith, and hope, contributes to the moral quality and merit of human acts. Additionally, human cooperation with God's grace is crucial for meritorious actions to take place. By recognizing the primacy of God's grace and actively cooperating with it, individuals can participate in the meritorious work that leads to the deservingness of rewards.

The Effects of Merit

Aquinas discusses the effects of merit. Merit refers to the deservingness of reward based on the moral quality of one's actions. Aquinas explores the various effects that merit has on the individual and identifies the following aspects:

Increase in Grace: One of the effects of merit is the increase in grace. Meritorious actions performed with the assistance of divine grace lead to a greater participation in the divine life. By freely cooperating with God's grace and performing good acts, individuals can grow in sanctifying grace, which strengthens their relationship with God and empowers them to live virtuously.

Increase in Charity: Merit also leads to an increase in charity, the theological virtue of divine love. As individuals perform acts of love and charity in a meritorious manner, their love for God and neighbor deepens. The more one engages in loving actions rooted in grace, the more their capacity for love expands and their charity grows.

Heavenly Reward: Merit prepares individuals for the reward of eternal life with God in heaven. Through their meritorious actions, individuals demonstrate their love for God and their commitment to living virtuously. In God's just judgment, He rewards these meritorious actions with the gift of eternal happiness and communion with Him in heaven.

Temporal Blessings: While the ultimate effect of merit is the heavenly reward, Aquinas also acknowledges that meritorious actions can have temporal blessings. These blessings may include various graces, virtues, and goods that contribute to an individual's flourishing in this life. However, Aquinas emphasizes that these temporal blessings should not be the primary focus or motive for meritorious actions, as the ultimate goal is the eternal reward.

Spiritual Growth and Perfection: Merit contributes to the spiritual growth and perfection of the individual. By actively cooperating with God's grace and living a life of virtue, individuals become more conformed to the image of Christ and grow in holiness. Meritorious actions, rooted in grace and performed with the right intention, have the transformative effect of shaping the character and virtues of the individual.

Aquinas's understanding of the effects of merit emphasizes the supernatural dimension of meritorious actions. Merit leads to an increase in grace and charity, prepares individuals for heavenly reward, and facilitates their spiritual growth and perfection. While temporal blessings

may accompany meritorious actions, they are
secondary to the ultimate goal of union with God
and eternal happiness in heaven.

The States of Life

Aquinas explores the various states of life and their respective duties and obligations. Key points are:

The Threefold Division: Aquinas divides the states of life into three categories: the state of perfection, the state of the active life, and the state of the contemplative life.

1. The State of Perfection: This refers to the religious or monastic life, where individuals commit themselves fully to God through vows of poverty, chastity, and obedience. Those in this state renounce worldly possessions, devote themselves to prayer, contemplation, and spiritual disciplines, and live in community under a rule or order.

2. The State of the Active Life: This includes the various secular vocations and occupations in which individuals engage in the affairs of the world while striving to live according to moral and virtuous principles. It encompasses roles such as marriage, parenthood, governance, and other professions or duties that involve active engagement with society and its concerns.

3. The State of the Contemplative Life: This refers to a more focused and dedicated pursuit of prayer, meditation, and contemplation. Individuals in this

state withdraw to a more solitary or secluded life, seeking deeper union with God through contemplation and spiritual exercises.

Duties and Obligations: Aquinas highlights the specific duties and obligations associated with each state of life. For example, in the state of perfection, religious individuals have obligations to live according to their vows, cultivate the virtues specific to their order, and engage in works of charity and spiritual growth. In the active life, individuals have duties toward their families, society, and their specific roles and responsibilities, such as providing for their loved ones, serving the common good, and pursuing justice. In the contemplative life, the focus is on prayer, study, and seeking spiritual union with God.

Complementary Nature: Aquinas emphasizes that these different states of life are complementary rather than contradictory. Each state contributes to the overall well-being of the Church and society, and all are necessary for the proper functioning of the body of Christ. The state of perfection, with its exclusive dedication to God, inspires and intercedes for the active and contemplative states. The active life engages with the world and brings the virtues of justice, charity, and prudence to bear on social and temporal matters. The contemplative life provides a witness to the primacy of the spiritual and fosters a deeper communion with God.

Aquinas recognizes that individuals are called to different states of life based on their unique gifts, inclinations, and divine providence. Each state has its own value and purpose, and individuals are encouraged to discern and embrace the state to which they are called, striving to fulfill their duties and obligations in accordance with God's will. The states of life offer a framework for individuals to live out their faith, serve others, and grow in holiness.

The Vows

A vow is a solemn promise or commitment made to God, binding oneself to perform a specific act or to live a certain way. Aquinas explores the nature, purpose, and effects of vows. Here are some key points regarding vows:

Definition of a Vow: Aquinas defines a vow as "a promise made to God about something that is within the power of the one making the vow". It is a deliberate and voluntary act of the will, expressing one's dedication and intention to fulfill a particular obligation or to abstain from something.

Objects of Vows: Vows can pertain to various aspects of human life, such as the practice of virtue, the pursuit of spiritual perfection, the renunciation of certain goods, or the performance of specific religious duties. For example, vows of poverty, chastity, and obedience are commonly taken by religious individuals in the state of perfection, while vows of fidelity and lifelong commitment are part of the sacrament of marriage.

Purpose of Vows: Vows serve as a means of expressing and strengthening one's devotion to God, as well as a way of offering oneself more fully to His service. They provide a structure and discipline for the spiritual life, helping individuals to grow in holiness and to overcome personal weaknesses or attachments. Vows also have the effect of binding the conscience, making it morally obligatory to fulfill the commitment made.

Conditions for a Valid Vow: Aquinas explains that for a vow to be valid, it must meet certain conditions. These include:

1. Knowledge and Consent: The person making the vow must have sufficient knowledge of what they are promising and the implications of their commitment. The vow must be made with deliberate and voluntary consent, without force or undue influence.

2. Lawful Matter: The content of the vow must be morally good and within the power of the person making the vow. It cannot involve anything contrary to God's law or the natural order.

3. Deliberate and Solemn Expression: The vow should be expressed deliberately and solemnly, indicating the seriousness and sacredness of the commitment. This may include appropriate rituals, prayers, or formulas.

Effects of Vows: Vows have several effects. They bind the person's conscience, making the fulfillment of the vow a moral obligation. They also establish a closer relationship between the person and God, as the vow signifies a deeper dedication and surrender to His will. Additionally, vows provide an opportunity for grace and merit, as individuals seek God's assistance in fulfilling their commitment and grow in virtue through their fidelity.

Aquinas emphasizes the importance of carefully discerning and reflecting upon the decision to make a vow. Vows should be made with prudence, sincerity, and a genuine desire to please God and grow in holiness. Fulfilling one's vows is a matter of faithfulness and integrity, and seeking the guidance and support of God's grace is crucial in living out the commitments made through vows.

The Virtues

Aquinas examines both the theological virtues (faith, hope, and charity) and the cardinal virtues (prudence, justice, fortitude, and temperance), along with other moral virtues.

The Theological Virtues:

1. Faith: Aquinas defines faith as the virtue by which we believe in God and all that He has revealed. It is a gift from God that enables us to assent to divine truths and trust in His promises.

2. Hope: Hope is the virtue by which we trust in God's promises for eternal life and rely on His grace to attain it. It gives us confidence in God's goodness and mercy.

3. Charity: Charity, also known as love, is the greatest of the virtues. It is the virtue by which we love God above all things and love our neighbors as ourselves. Charity perfects all other virtues and directs our actions toward the ultimate end of union with God.

The Cardinal Virtues:

1. Prudence: Prudence is the virtue that enables us to discern what is good and to choose the right

means to achieve it. It involves practical wisdom, sound judgment, and the ability to make morally upright decisions.

2. Justice: Justice is the virtue that inclines us to give each person their due. It involves fairness, equity, and respecting the rights and dignity of others.

3. Fortitude: Fortitude is the virtue of courage and strength in facing difficulties, dangers, and temptations. It enables us to persevere in pursuing the good, even in the face of obstacles or opposition.

4. Temperance: Temperance is the virtue that moderates our desires and appetites, ensuring they are in line with reason and guided by self-control. It helps us avoid excess and maintain balance in our actions.

Other Moral Virtues:

Aquinas also discusses various moral virtues that relate to specific aspects of human behavior and character. These virtues include humility, honesty, patience, kindness, generosity, chastity, meekness, and many others. These virtues contribute to the formation of a virtuous character and guide our actions in specific areas of life.

Aquinas emphasizes that virtues are acquired through habituation and practice. By repeatedly choosing virtuous actions, we develop virtuous habits that shape our character. Through the grace of God and our cooperation, we grow in virtue and become more aligned with the moral perfection exemplified by Christ.

Aquinas' discussion of the virtues provides a comprehensive understanding of moral and spiritual development, highlighting the importance of cultivating virtues to live a virtuous and fulfilling life in accordance with God's will. The virtues enable us to align our actions with the divine order and strive for holiness.

The Gifts of the Holy Spirit

The gifts of the Holy Spirit are special graces bestowed by God to assist individuals in living a virtuous and holy life. Aquinas identifies seven gifts, which are traditionally based on the prophecy of Isaiah 11:2-3:

Wisdom: The gift of wisdom enables a person to have a deep understanding and appreciation of divine truths and to judge and order all things according to their proper value in light of God's perspective.

Understanding: The gift of understanding grants insight into the meaning and significance of revealed truths. It helps one to grasp the mysteries of faith and to see how they relate to one's own life and the world around them.

Counsel (Right Judgment): The gift of counsel, also known as right judgment, assists in making prudent decisions and choosing the right course of action in various situations. It guides individuals to act in accordance with God's will and the moral teachings of the Church.

Fortitude (Courage): The gift of fortitude, or courage, strengthens a person to overcome obstacles, persevere in the face of difficulties, and endure suffering for the sake of righteousness. It empowers individuals to stand firm in their faith and to live virtuously even in challenging circumstances.

Knowledge: The gift of knowledge allows individuals to have a deeper understanding of created things in relation to God. It helps one to discern the proper use and value of created goods and to see how they point to their Creator.

Piety (Reverence): The gift of piety, also referred to as reverence, instills in a person a deep reverence and love for God, as well as respect and honor for others and for the sacred. It inspires acts of worship, devotion, and respectful conduct.

Fear of the Lord (Wonder and Awe): The gift of fear of the Lord, also known as wonder and awe, engenders a profound sense of reverence, humility, and awe in the presence of God. It moves individuals to avoid sin and to embrace a sincere desire to please and obey God out of love.

These gifts are infused into the souls of the faithful through the Holy Spirit and are intended to complement and perfect the virtues. They enable individuals to live in a closer union with God, to discern His will, and to grow in holiness. By cooperating with the gifts of the Holy Spirit, individuals are empowered to live a life guided by

God's grace and to bear spiritual fruit for the
benefit of themselves and others.

The Beatitudes

The Beatitudes are a set of blessings proclaimed by Jesus in His Sermon on the Mount (Matthew 5:3-12) and serve as guidelines for attaining happiness and blessedness in this life and the life to come. Aquinas examines each of the Beatitudes individually, highlighting their spiritual significance and moral implications.

Blessed are the poor in spirit: This refers to those who recognize their spiritual poverty and dependency on God. They are detached from worldly possessions and are open to receiving the Kingdom of Heaven.

Blessed are those who mourn: These are individuals who grieve over their sins and the brokenness of the world. They find comfort and solace in God's mercy and the hope of eternal consolation.

Blessed are the meek: The meek are those who are humble, gentle, and patient. They submit to God's will and trust in His providence, finding their strength in Him.

Blessed are those who hunger and thirst for righteousness: These individuals have a deep longing and desire for righteousness and justice.

They strive to live in accordance with God's commandments and seek to establish His Kingdom on earth.

Blessed are the merciful: The merciful show compassion, forgiveness, and kindness to others. They imitate God's mercy and are promised to receive mercy in return.

Blessed are the pure in heart: The pure in heart are those who possess sincerity, integrity, and a single-hearted devotion to God. They seek to love God above all else and are granted the vision of God.

Blessed are the peacemakers: Peacemakers work to reconcile differences, promote harmony, and establish peace in their relationships and communities. They reflect the image of God as the ultimate peacemaker.

Blessed are those who are persecuted for righteousness' sake: These individuals face opposition, ridicule, and persecution because of their commitment to righteousness and fidelity to God. They are promised the reward of the Kingdom of Heaven.

The Fruits of the Holy Spirit

The concept of the Fruits of the Holy Spirit is derived from the Bible, particularly from the writings of St. Paul in his letter to the Galatians (Galatians 5:22-23). The Fruits of the Holy Spirit refer to the virtues and qualities that are produced in the lives of individuals who are guided and empowered by the Holy Spirit.

The Fruits of the Holy Spirit, as listed by St. Paul, are:

Love (Charity): Love is the greatest virtue and encompasses selflessness, compassion, and care for others. It is a self-giving love that seeks the well-being of others.

Joy: Joy is a deep and abiding sense of gladness that is rooted in one's relationship with God. It transcends circumstances and is not dependent on external factors.

Peace: Peace is the inner tranquility and harmony that comes from being reconciled with God. It also involves promoting peace in relationships and society.

Patience: Patience is the ability to endure and remain steadfast in the face of difficulties, trials, or delays. It involves forbearance and a willingness to wait for God's timing.

Kindness: Kindness is the quality of being considerate, compassionate, and gentle towards others. It involves acts of goodwill and benevolence.

Goodness: Goodness refers to moral excellence and virtue. It involves doing what is right and acting in accordance with God's will.

Faithfulness: Faithfulness is being reliable, trustworthy, and steadfast in one's commitments. It involves being faithful to God and to others.

Gentleness: Gentleness is the quality of being mild-mannered, humble, and considerate in one's interactions. It involves treating others with kindness and respect.

Self-control: Self-control is the ability to govern one's desires, impulses, and actions. It involves discipline and moderation in all areas of life.

These Fruits of the Holy Spirit are seen as the natural outgrowth of a life that is deeply connected to and guided by the Holy Spirit. They reflect the transformation that takes place in the lives of believers as they cooperate with the work of the Holy Spirit and allow Him to shape their character and behavior. The Fruits of the Holy Spirit are not produced through mere human effort, but through the supernatural work of the Holy Spirit within the hearts of individuals.

The Works of Mercy

The Works of Mercy, also known as the Corporal and Spiritual Works of Mercy, are acts of charity and compassion towards others that are rooted in Christian teachings. They are considered important ways to express love for one's neighbor and to follow the example of Jesus Christ. The Works of Mercy are traditionally divided into two categories: Corporal Works of Mercy and Spiritual Works of Mercy.

The Corporal Works of Mercy are focused on meeting the physical and material needs of others. They include:

Feeding the hungry: Providing food and sustenance to those who are hungry and in need.

Giving drink to the thirsty: Providing clean water and refreshment to those who are thirsty or lack access to safe drinking water.

Clothing the naked: Offering clothing and covering to those who lack adequate clothing or are in need of warmth.

Sheltering the homeless: Providing shelter and housing to those who are homeless or lack a safe place to live.

Visiting the sick: Offering care, comfort, and companionship to those who are ill or confined due to illness or disability.

Visiting the imprisoned: Offering support, encouragement, and spiritual guidance to those who are in prison or detention.

Burying the dead: Showing respect and providing assistance in the burial and funeral arrangements for the deceased, and offering comfort to those who are grieving.

The Spiritual Works of Mercy are focused on meeting the spiritual and emotional needs of others. They include:

Instructing the ignorant: Sharing knowledge, wisdom, and guidance with those who lack understanding, particularly in matters of faith and morals.

Counseling the doubtful: Offering support, encouragement, and guidance to those who are experiencing doubt or uncertainty in their faith or life circumstances.

Admonishing sinners: Lovingly correcting and guiding others who have fallen into sin, with the intention of helping them turn back to God and live a virtuous life.

Bearing wrongs patiently: Practicing patience, forgiveness, and forbearance when faced with the faults, offenses, or injustices of others.

Forgiving offenses willingly: Extending forgiveness and reconciliation to those who have hurt or wronged us, just as God forgives us.

Comforting the afflicted: Providing solace, compassion, and emotional support to those who are experiencing sorrow, grief, or other forms of suffering.

Praying for the living and the dead: Offering prayers and intercession for the needs and intentions of others, both the living and those who have passed away.

The Works of Mercy are considered essential expressions of Christian love and discipleship. By engaging in these acts of charity and compassion, believers seek to imitate Christ and bring His love and mercy to those in need. They serve as a practical application of the Christian faith and a tangible way to extend God's grace and compassion to others.

Astrology

Aquinas acknowledges the existence of astrology and recognizes that people have believed in its influence on human affairs based on celestial bodies such as the movements of the stars and planets. However, he approaches the subject with caution and skepticism, particularly in relation to predicting specific individual events and personal characteristics solely based on astrological charts.

Aquinas argues that astrology's claims of determining individual destinies or character traits are not supported by sound reasoning. He emphasizes that human beings possess free will, and their actions and choices are not entirely determined by external celestial influences. Aquinas firmly upholds the role of human freedom and moral responsibility, affirming that individuals have the capacity to make choices independent of astrological determinism.

Furthermore, Aquinas challenges the notion that celestial bodies directly cause events in the world. He posits that the celestial bodies' movements are governed by natural causes and are not directly involved in the affairs of human beings or individual events.

While Aquinas does not outright dismiss astrology entirely, he expresses skepticism about its accuracy and limitations. He encourages individuals to prioritize moral virtues, prudence, and reliance on divine providence rather than relying solely on astrological predictions.

It's important to note that Aquinas wrote within the historical context of his time, and his views on astrology reflect the prevailing attitudes of the medieval period. Today, astrology is often approached and evaluated through different lenses, including scientific, psychological, and cultural perspectives.

Ultimately, Aquinas's engagement with astrology in the 'Summa Theologica' reflects his attempt to reconcile popular beliefs of his time with the broader theological and philosophical framework he develops throughout his work.

Thomas Aquinas' Ethics

Ethics is a significant aspect of Aquinas' work, particularly in the second part of the 'Summa Theologica' called the 'Secunda Secundae' or the 'Treatise on Human Acts.' In this section, Aquinas addresses various moral issues and provides a framework for ethical decision-making that never aged and still holds true today.

Aquinas' ethical system is deeply rooted in his understanding of human nature, the purpose of human life, and the pursuit of the ultimate good, which he identifies as union with God. He argues that human beings are rational creatures, endowed with intellect and free will, and are called to live a life of virtue in accordance with reason and God's moral law.

Aquinas distinguishes three levels of moral actions:
1. Intrinsically good actions, such as acts of charity or justice, which are always good in themselves;
2. Actions that are morally indifferent or neutral, meaning they are neither good nor evil in themselves, such as everyday activities that do not have moral significance;
3. Intrinsically evil actions, which are always morally wrong, such as stealing, lying or murder.

Aquinas also introduces the concept of virtues, which he categorizes into two types:
Theological and cardinal.
The theological virtues (faith, hope, and charity) are infused by God and orient humans toward their ultimate end, which is union with God.
The cardinal virtues (prudence, justice, fortitude, and temperance) are acquired virtues that help individuals develop moral character and live a virtuous life.

Prudence, in particular, is highly emphasized by Aquinas. It is considered the 'mother' of all virtues as it guides individuals in making sound moral judgments and choosing the right course of action. Aquinas also discusses various moral topics such as sin, conscience, natural law, and the moral evaluation of specific actions.

Pursuit of peace: Aquinas emphasizes the importance of pursuing peace and avoiding violence whenever possible. In the case of a potential world war, his teachings encourage individuals, communities, and nations to actively seek peaceful resolutions, promote dialogue, and engage in diplomatic efforts to prevent or mitigate conflicts.

'Just' war principles: Aquinas' ethical framework includes principles that govern the morality of engaging in war when all peaceful options have been exhausted. The principles of just war theory, such as legitimate authority, just cause, proportionality, and reasonable chance of success, can provide a framework for evaluating the ethical implications of a potential war. Applying these principles can help individuals assess the justifiability of engaging in conflict and guide decision-making.

Human rights and dignity: Aquinas' emphasis on the inherent dignity and rights of every human person can inform the ethical considerations in the face of war. The principles of justice, fairness, and respect for human life and dignity should guide actions, policies, and decisions. Protecting innocent civilians, upholding human rights, and minimizing harm to non-combatants are ethical imperatives even in the midst of conflict.

Moral responsibility: Aquinas teaches that individuals have moral responsibilities not only to themselves but also to the wider community and society. In the context of a potential world war, recognizing the interconnectedness of nations and the shared responsibility for maintaining peace can be a guiding principle. Promoting cooperation, dialogue, and international collaboration becomes crucial for preventing conflicts and working towards peaceful resolutions.

Overall, Aquinas' ethical framework in the 'Summa Theologica' emphasizes the importance of reason, virtues, and the pursuit of the ultimate good in guiding human behavior and decision-making. His approach has had a profound influence on Catholic moral theology and continues to be studied and discussed by theologians and philosophers today.

www.ingramcontent.com/pod-product-compliance
Lightning Source LLC
Chambersburg PA
CBHW031430150726
47989CB00002B/890